Finding My Professional Heart

A brief guide to compassionate care and mindfulness for practitioners

Natius Oelofsen

Lantern

ISBN: 978 1 908625 40 3

First published in 2016 by Lantern Publishing Ltd

Lantern Publishing Ltd, The Old Hayloft, Vantage Business Park, Bloxham Rd, Banbury, OX16 9UX, UK

www.lanternpublishing.com

British Library Cataloguing in Publication Data

A catalogue record for this book is available from the British Library

The authors and publisher have made every attempt to ensure the content of this book is up to date and accurate. However, healthcare knowledge and information is changing all the time so the reader is advised to double-check any information in this text on drug usage, treatment procedures, the use of equipment, etc. to confirm that it complies with the latest safety recommendations, standards of practice and legislation, as well as local Trust policies and procedures. Students are advised to check with their tutor and/or mentor before carrying out any of the procedures in this textbook.

Cover design by Andrew Magee Design Ltd

Printed in the UK

CONTENTS

PREFACE

I've learned that people will forget what you said, people will forget what you did, but people will never forget how you made them feel.

—Maya Angelou

This little book is written for people who are passionate about health and social care services for vulnerable people. I believe that many of the changes in recent decades in the ways that health and social care services are commissioned, while bringing about efficiencies in the delivery of care, also have unintended consequences. One of the most damaging of these is that we have commodified and "codified" service delivery to such an extent that we have lost some of the human touch. We seem to have forgotten that care and treatment is fundamentally delivered through human encounters, despite the advanced technologies that may underpin the processes or procedures at hand.

We can see this in how we teach students competencies and procedures, rather than how to be with people who are vulnerable or in distress. And in the ways in which daily clinical and care practices have been diluted by contracting requirements that lead to practitioners spending disproportionate amounts of their time collecting and capturing data instead of delivering care. Most tragically, some recent reports into failings within health and social care systems, such as the report into Mid Staffordshire hospital in the United Kingdom by Lord Francis, showed just how far things can go wrong when whole care systems become so focused on their "performance" that they lose sight of their core purpose – delivering care with humanity and compassion.

In the wake of the Francis report in the NHS, and other, similar reports into failings in our care systems, we have implemented many procedural and regulatory changes. We have introduced inspection regimes and various legal responsibilities that aim to increase accountability and scrutiny. Politicians and heads of governing bodies delivered speeches and wrote lengthy policy documents containing terms such as increasing accountability, strengthening governance, and changing cultures. But none of these efforts, however worthy they are, will truly solve the problems we face without a fresh acknowledgement of the human element that permeates all of the work at the front line within health and social care. I am not thinking here about the "human factors" that play a role when things go wrong, important as those may be, but more about the human factors that colour and shape the encounters between nurses and their patients, support workers and their service users, or social workers and their "cases".

Do we really acknowledge that this work involves more than the nurse taking a measurement or administering an injection? Do we truly understand that he is exposed to a frightened person who might be in pain or in fear of suffering from a serious illness? Do we understand that the support worker not only provides a point of contact with the service, but also functions as a friend and a sounding board in the face of loneliness and despair? In turn, the social worker, while arranging practical support for someone, may also become the focus of their fear of the future – will my child be removed? – or their suffering that might stem from past trauma.

As these examples illustrate, care and healing involve human encounters. And these encounters have an impact on both service recipients and practitioners. I contend that, when practitioners are faced with others' trauma, need, and vulnerability, in order to deliver truly effective help that addresses the core issues, it is important that they remain in touch with the humanity of the people they work with – *and their own*! But this is difficult, as we are social beings and exposure to someone else's need or vulnerability is likely to sensitise us to our own. This, in turn, can be a frightening and anxiety-inducing process. It is therefore tempting to distance ourselves from the human being in front of us and focus on the task at hand. Time pressure and bureaucracy make this distancing defence so very easy. Truly compassionate care, on the other hand, provides us with a way to stay in touch with our professional hearts, while treating the other as a fellow human being.

Far from being just a personal defence, however, wards, teams, services and large systems can develop institutionalised defences against anxiety. These often take the form of strict hierarchies, multiple policies and procedures, as well as "unofficial" distancing defences; for instance, members of staff groups can develop rigid and negative attitudes towards other staff groups or agencies, as Isabel Menzies-Lyth found in her well-known study of a district teaching hospital back in the 1950s (Menzies-Lyth, 1990).

Thinking again about the many "bureaucratic intrusions" on the care process so prevalent nowadays, I believe that there has never been a time when it was so easy to lose sight of the human needs of the people who make use of the services we are contracted to deliver. This, for me, and, hopefully for you too, is compelling reason to focus our attention on ensuring that compassion and humanity find their way back to the centre of care.

In the rest of this small book, I would like to offer you a way to channel your efforts to achieve this in your own practice. Readers with an interest in academic research may be aware that the academic study of compassion is still in its infancy. Recent years saw an increase in the amount of research in this area, primarily due to advances in brain imaging technology and their application to neuroscience and psychology research.

In contrast, much of what we understand about compassion originates in the ancient wisdom of contemplative traditions that can be found in most of the major world religions. To help explain some of the ideas in this book, I turned to both of these sources. In the pages that follow you will find a mixture of ideas ranging from a neuropsychological model of compassionate mind, to parables from the Bible and ideas from Buddhism. The examples and ideas chosen were selected simply because I thought they illustrated the points in question rather well, and – quite obviously – because I was aware of them. There are most likely many equally valid ideas from other traditions that would serve the purpose equally well and readers are welcome to send in their own examples to me at the address given below.

As we shall see a little later, compassion is more a way of life than a trait. What is often hardest for practitioners to accept is that compassion with the suffering of others is contingent with our ability to approach ourselves compassionately as suffering beings each one in our own right. And, probably most importantly, compassion is not a competency, something that we can train ourselves to be; it is to be cultivated and nurtured every day through self-discipline, engaging in compassion-enhancing practices, and in taking care of our suffering selves.

In the next chapter, I would like to start you off on your journey towards a compassionate life by offering you an overview of the concept of compassion that encompasses modern as well as ancient perspectives. *Chapter 2* considers some ideas on how to become compassionate and discusses the enemies of compassion. *Chapter 3* provides a small sample of some scientific research into compassion and presents an overview of a neuroscience-based model of compassion. *Chapter 4* explores the links between mindfulness and compassion. *Chapter 5* provides some guidelines and a road map for cultivating a compassionate outlook and approach, while the *Appendix* offers a set of meditations and practices that you can use along the way. In the process, you will develop a deeper understanding of what compassion is and the healing power that compassionate approaches can offer us both personally and professionally. You will also encounter some ideas on how compassion "works" in practice. I hope that you will find all of these ideas engaging and inspirational. But most of all I hope that you will be inspired to embark on, and sustain the journey towards becoming a compassionate practitioner that this little volume offers.

Finally, I would like to encourage readers to contact me with their comments and ideas. If you have any feedback on this little book, please contact me via Lantern Publishing at the following email address: info@lanternpublishing.com.

01
COMPASSION

Too often we underestimate the power of a touch, a smile, a kind word, a listening ear, an honest compliment, or the smallest act of caring, all of which have the potential to turn a life around.

— Leo Buscaglia

What do you think is meant by the term "compassionate care"? Can you illustrate this with an example from your own area of practice? The following words or phrases are frequently used to describe ideas similar to compassion. Consider the meaning of each and see if you can think of some ways in which they differ from your understanding of true compassion.

- Empathy
- Feeling sorry for someone
- Pity
- Kindness
- Understanding how someone feels through personal experience
- Feeling drawn to, or close to a client or service user.

What are the implications of these differences for your practice? (It might be interesting to return to this question once you have read the rest of this book and see if your answers have changed.)

In recent years the term "compassionate care" has become something of a buzzword in the health and social care systems of the United Kingdom. As was mentioned above, this followed a number of high profile scandals where staff in settings such as hospitals and care homes were found to have shown an almost incredible lack of kindness towards very vulnerable people in their care.

Investigations into these incidents led to long and complex reports, such as the report by Lord Robert Francis, QC, into the failures of care in Mid-Staffordshire (Francis, 2013). Lord Francis made many recommendations. He indicated that organisational culture in the NHS needs to change: Staff at all levels need to be held more accountable for the care they deliver or oversee. And, most importantly, patients should be placed at the centre of their care across all aspects of the work of the NHS.

I hope that this might mean that we are getting back to basics: at the heart of health and social care is a healing encounter between people. Delivering care with compassion means that we work with people in ways that respect their humanity and that we place "ticking boxes" lower on the priority list than showing caring and kindness towards the recipients of our services.

What might the conflicts be between "ticking boxes" (and other bureaucratic intrusions) and care with compassion, in your setting?

Here are some issues that professionals have come up with when asked this question:

- Work pressure.
- Meeting targets for productivity – GPs, for example, often say that they have less than 10 minutes per consultation.
- Making sure that the correct paperwork and forms are completed.
- Too few staff on duty.
- The conflict between delivering what care recipients need and the services that are actually commissioned.
- Delivering services in the form of discrete tasks, rather than engaging with vulnerable and distressed people to form caring relationships. (This can be described as task-based vs. relationship-based care.)

When you are under stress, what are the possible obstacles to compassionate human encounters in your care setting? For example, might you be less willing to listen to people, or perhaps less friendly, or more easily irritated? What might the impact be on the experiences that users of your service have with you? What about the possibility that the quality of care might be affected?

Compassionate care has been defined as "intelligent kindness" (NHS Commissioning Board, 2012). Examining this phrase, the kindness element refers to the "human" dimension, but there is also an "intelligent" component. Compassion is kindness directed through the complex processes of professional (clinical) reasoning and ethics; to be compassionate is to be intelligently helpful. The *personal* – your humanity – and the *professional* – your knowledge and skills – meet up in delivering care with compassion.

Think about this for a moment.

In your training and in your day-to-day encounters at work, how prominent is the human dimension of your work, compared to technical and administrative dimensions? Few people enter caring professions with an intense desire to collect patient data or to spend hours recording notes! Instead, a strong motivation to help others who are vulnerable is probably a much more common driving force. Why do you get out of bed in the morning?

Yet, our professional training tends to teach us how to deliver care professionally and competently, but not how to be with people who are suffering while delivering that care. However, we **are** with suffering or vulnerable people and, unless we acknowledge their impact on us and our impact on them, we are heading for troubled waters (Stokoe, 2011).

The training of care professionals across health and social care in anglophone countries focuses so much on technical competence (the tasks relating to providing a service) that we find it difficult to think and talk about the human dimensions of care. This difficulty is reflected in the ways we have set up the systems through which we deliver care in large hospitals, mental health teams, and social care agencies. Nurses, doctors, therapists and social workers are constantly confronted with high levels of need and vulnerability in the people they work with, yet bereft of opportunities to explore, reflect, and talk about the impact of delivering care on them as human beings. The natural human response to being confronted with others' vulnerability is to start fearing for our own. Where is that "contained"? If not acknowledged and dealt with openly, practitioners can turn away from their own internal pain and by doing so, become unable to show compassion for the pain of people using their services.

As mentioned in the preface, this lack of acknowledgement of the human impact of delivering care can also lead to institutionalised defences against anxiety such as strict systems and rules, hierarchies, and rigidly set ways of doing things. These defences protect staff against the impact of others' distress on them (Menzies-Lyth, 1990).

Finding a language for the human dimension of care

Social pedagogues – social care professionals who mainly work in continental Europe and Scandinavia – talk about the head, heart and hands (Stephens, 2013). Using this metaphor, effective and frequently commended practice, often emphasise head and hands over heart. Yet it is the *heart* that makes all the difference. The language of compassion provides us with an opportunity to talk openly about our professional hearts, and to give heart-based practice the prominent place it deserves both in our *practice*, and in our *thinking* about the work we do. In our compassion, we restore the balance between technical competence and the human dimension of what we do.

This book considers questions of the professional heart such as the following: What does compassion really mean? How do you sustain working from the heart (compassion) when you have a high workload, limited resources, and many – often conflicting – demands on your time? How do you develop yourself as a compassionate practitioner? And even, is there an evidence base or theory of compassion?

Expanding the definition of compassion

We have seen compassion defined by the Chief Nursing Officer in the UK as "intelligent kindness" (NHS Commissioning Board, 2012, p13). A more traditional definition is given by psychologist Paul Gilbert, following the Dalai Lama's teaching, that compassion is a keen awareness of the suffering of others coupled with a strong wish to ameliorate it (Gilbert, 2010).

Both of these definitions of compassion convey the sense that compassion has a strong emotional component. Yet compassion is not pity or feeling sorry for someone. The emotional dimension of compassion serves to motivate compassionate action, so that compassion can be seen as a way to turn a certain type of emotion into action.

Many of the world's major religions and spiritual traditions contain within their collective wisdom rich and interesting ideas about compassion. For example, Buddhism emphasises the intentional and active elements of compassion to such an extent that compassion is viewed as both a way of being and a way of living (Hangartner, 2013). I will refer to ideas from some of these traditions later on, especially contemplative traditions such as Buddhism and various forms of meditation.

A key question about compassion

Can anyone be compassionate? Are some people more prone to compassion than others? Are there some individuals who simply cannot be compassionate, no matter how hard they try? For services and agencies that deliver care to vulnerable people, this should be a key question. If compassion cannot be acquired in some way, then can you somehow assess how compassionate people are and only recruit staff that shows the requisite compassion levels for the job at hand? Can you train individuals to be more compassionate or target compassionate behaviour as part of monitoring services' performance? All these ideas – with their adherents and detractors – featured in recent debates within the UK context, following the series of scandals in care settings mentioned earlier.

Whether compassion can be measured and assessed, targeted as a key performance indicator, or trained in a classroom are moot points. What we do know about compassion suggests a somewhat different understanding of how compassion can be developed and sustained in people. The knowledge we draw on here arose over many centuries in the contemplative traditions of the great world religions. However, since the 1960s many of these ideas have made their way into Western academic circles, and are now starting to be subjected to investigation by researchers schooled in modern scientific methods. In fact, some of the research cited below used the latest technologies such as MRI brain scans. The result is that we now have several neuroscientifically informed models of compassion, one of which we will discuss below.

With these data as evidence, the following chapters explore the nature of compassion, how it can be developed, and how we are starting to understand the impact and power of compassion better through cutting-edge scientific research.

For reflection...

In this chapter I argued that the language of compassion can help us think and talk about the human dimension of caregiving in ways that can serve to enable us to deliver compassionate care in practice. We have started our journey towards understanding compassion by briefly examining two definitions of compassion, the first considering compassion to be awareness of another's suffering combined with a desire to alleviate it, and the second viewing compassion as intelligent kindness. Take a few moments to think about the different facets of compassion these definitions have highlighted:

- Compassion as awareness of suffering.
- Compassion as an intention to alleviate suffering.
- Compassion as kindness directed by "intelligence".

Can you think of examples where you were the recipient of compassion in accordance with any of the above?

02

HOW TO BECOME COMPASSIONATE

Compassion hurts. When you feel connected to everything,
you also feel responsible for everything.

— Andrew Boyd

Take a moment to think of your day-to-day tasks in your work role. Do you work directly with people who are vulnerable and in need of services? Are you a decision maker in a context linked with services to vulnerable people? Can you define your sphere of influence?

Now try to make a list of behaviours or attitudes that fall within the realm of possibility for you at work that would reflect a compassionate approach. You could list key tasks or small things that would reflect your compassion. It could be that you stop yourself from saying, "Oh no, not him again," about a dependent service user who left a message for you to return, and instead respond to the person as if it was the first time they called. You could think of going the extra mile for someone requesting your help. It could even be that you decide to advocate a little more strongly for a vulnerable group in a high-powered meeting you are due to attend. What would constitute compassionate acts, behaviours or attitudes within your sphere of influence?

Finally, I wonder what your thoughts are about how someone can become compassionate, when you consider all three aspects of compassion we discussed in the previous chapter: intelligent kindness, awareness of suffering, and an intention to ameliorate suffering? What do you think are the components guiding the development of compassion in individuals?

Growing your compassionate self: an agricultural metaphor

The contemplative traditions mentioned earlier believe that compassion cannot be targeted or directly trained, but it can be *cultivated*. What does that mean? A reasonable analogy is to consider compassion to develop in ways that are similar to cultivating a plant. For a plant to grow and thrive, you might need to enrich the soil, supply essential nutrients and water, and add heat and light. You may also need to provide protection from unfavourable conditions such as frost, flooding, or pests. But essentially, the seed would germinate, and the seedling would grow, driven by its own natural life force. The plant itself would thrive, in large part thanks to being provided with the right conditions to support its growth and development. Cultivating compassion follows a similar process, the first part of which involves setting in place the right pre-conditions to allow the compassionate parts of human nature to emerge and to flourish.

Pushing the above analogy a little further, a tiny seed can become a large tree that gives habitat and shade to many creatures. But in order for the seed to become the source of life or comfort to other creatures, its process has to start from within – it first germinates and then grows. Focusing inwards to unlock its own nature allows it to emerge as a blessing to other creatures (see the "parable of the mustard seed", Matthew 13:31–32 in the Bible). This too is an essential aspect of compassion.

Another well-known story about compassion illustrates the nature of compassion a little more: the parable of the Good Samaritan, one of the best known of the Biblical parables (Luke 10: 25–37), relates the story of a Jewish man who was travelling on the road between Jerusalem and Jericho when he fell victim to an ambush and was beaten, robbed and left for dead by the side of the road. A priest and some religious scholars passed by along the road and ignored his plight, but a Samaritan – a group that was not well liked by the Jews of the time – took pity on the man, helped him to an inn, and paid for his care without wanting anything in return.

Below we discuss an interesting research study that used this parable as its inspiration, but for the purposes of this discussion, there is an important aspect of compassion illustrated by the contrasting actions of the priest and religious scholars on the one hand, and the Samaritan on the other: in compassionate terms, the former went about their business *in the usual way*, whilst the latter *really saw* the wounded man and noticed his plight, and then he acted to alleviate his suffering. One of the key characteristics of any act of true compassion is that the compassionate individual really notices the other's suffering. Before you can act compassionately, you need to pay attention and be alert to the suffering of the other.

Cultivating compassion therefore involves cultivating the capability to pay close attention, alongside an intention to alleviate suffering. This intention – the second key aspect – draws on many

11

fundamental aspects of our humanity, including our ethics, values, sense of self and our view of the world.

The third key aspect, illustrated by the Good Samaritan story, is that of compassionate *action* – compassion is not about just feeling sad or sorry for someone else, but about making an active and practical difference. So compassion joins together three key elements that are integral to our humanity:

1. Awareness of the suffering of another (really noticing/paying attention)
2. Intention to make a difference: ethics, values, sense of self; and
3. Taking action, actively making a difference.

These three elements of compassion integrate our internal sense of identity and self, our prosocial orientation (focus on others), and our capacity to act on the world. For me, this way of thinking about compassion also explains why compassion is better viewed as an enduring way of life (or *orientation* to life) than as a series of one off events or kind deeds (Bornemann & Singer, 2013). It also highlights the areas we might need to address should we wish to cultivate compassion in ourselves and in our professional practices.

Taking your cue from the parable of the Good Samaritan mentioned here, can you come up with a compassion story of your own? Think of an incident or an event where someone showed you real compassion. Which of the components of compassion mentioned above were most clearly present in the other person's approach? How did they notice your suffering at that moment? How did they express their intention to make a difference, and how did their actions help?

Can you think of a time when you were really compassionate towards someone else? It does not have to be a major incident and you need not be the hero, but it could be a really small event, e.g. letting someone step into the queue in front of you at the supermarket as you noticed that they seemed to be stressed and in a rush, or offering to give directions to someone who appeared lost on the street in your home town.

What can you learn from thinking about these stories in terms of the components of compassion mentioned above?

Enemies of compassion

Compassion is vulnerable. Once cultivated, the conditions that allow it to flourish need to be maintained. This includes guarding against what can be referred to as the enemies of compassion – motivations and attitudes that counteract the compassionate heart of helping behaviour.

For example, cruelty is the antithesis of compassion. But compassion also has subtler enemies such as pity and despair (Hangartner, 2013). These emotions are not conducive to compassionate action; instead, the distress they cause is likely to lead us to develop defences of emotional distancing from the suffering of others (Menzies-Lyth, 1990). I can easily imagine the religious scholars and Priest in the Good Samaritan story above hurrying past the suffering man, reminding themselves, "There but for the grace of God go I."

The idea of compassionate intent, or loving kindness in the Buddhist tradition, also has its enemies, namely attachment and desire (Hangartner, 2013). These represent dangers as, at their core, they are self-referential. The Samaritan, in the story, paid for the man's care at the inn and left, allowing him to go on his way without a sense of obligation to his benefactor.

Attachment and desire focus on binding others to ourselves and, for recipients of kindness, create spiritual debts or a sense of obligation. The kindness in compassion is at its essence about letting someone proceed on *their* journey stronger than before, rather than holding them back indebted to us by their gratitude or a sense of obligation.

Perhaps it is therefore also important to add a fourth dimension to the core components of compassion discussed above, namely the ability to let go of someone you have been compassionate to. This, in traditional Buddhism, is referred to as equanimity (Jinananda, 2012). It is believed that without equanimity, we tend to "hold on" to emotions and people in ways that increase our suffering. Equanimity means that we do not allow anger, lack of forgiveness, and desire to drive our motivations and behaviour. It does not involve denying our pain, but it involves awareness with acceptance, without "holding on". In the Chapter on mindfulness below, we will consider similar ideas about the mental processes we experience from day to day.

"From Jerusalem to Jericho": the Princeton experiment

As a final illustration of how vulnerable the compassionate way can be, let us consider the power of context as illustrated by a famous experiment in social psychology, conducted a number of decades ago. "From Jerusalem to Jericho" was a study done in the early 1970s at Princeton University to investigate the relevance of dispositional and situational variables in helping behaviour (Darley & Batson, 1973).

The researchers recruited subjects from among theological seminary students (i.e. students who were following advanced postgraduate studies in theology). The participants were split into two main groups. The first group was to prepare and deliver a short talk on the various careers and job opportunities for seminary graduates and the second main group was to talk on "The Good Samaritan" parable from the Bible. The students were asked to report to the researchers at a certain location on campus and given instructions on where to go and give their talks. Unknown to the students, the researchers organised for a collaborator to place himself along the route to the venue for the participants' talk. The collaborator was shabbily dressed and slumped over and, as the participants passed by, coughed and groaned.

The two groups of students were also split into further subgroups which were placed under varying degrees of time pressure by the researchers. Time pressure was the "situational" variable. The "dispositional" variables tested were the degree and kind of religiosity shown by participants. Stopping, helping and the kinds of help offered were assessed as the outcome or "dependent" variables.

When the results came in, the researchers were quite surprised that participants' degree of religiosity did not predict significantly who stopped to help the victim. Neither did the topic of the students' proposed talks make a difference. So, asking the students to think about possible post-qualification career opportunities as against an act of compassion did not make a significant difference in whether or not someone stopped to help. Instead, the only variable that made a significant and consistent difference was the one measuring time pressure. Those under pressure to give their talk, as the programme had a tight deadline, were less likely to stop and help than those who were not under time pressure, irrespective of how religious they were or of the topic of their talks.

Were you surprised by the results of the Good Samaritan experiment mentioned above? What would you have expected the outcome to be? In a recent group discussion, I was surprised to find that the students expected the less religious seminary students to be more compassionate. Do you think the outcome of this experiment would be different if conducted today?

For reflection...

In this chapter we uncovered four key aspects of compassion that could be seen as key features of any act of true compassion; namely, really noticing someone's suffering, an intention to alleviate it, compassionate action, and the ability to truly let go. Binding others to ourselves through acts of kindness does not constitute true compassion. Respecting the other's journey and focusing your actions on ways that would help them along on their own journeys differentiate acts of kindness from acts of compassion. What does "letting go" mean to you personally and in the context of your role? Is this something that comes easily, or something that is really difficult for you or your team?

Consider contextual factors that could be enemies of compassion. What do the results of the Darley and Batson experiment indicate to you about the role of such factors as time pressure and work demands as potential enemies of compassion in your setting? What is needed to restore the balance?

INTERLUDE
THE FOUR PILLARS
OF COMPASSION

In the previous two chapters, we explored the definition and nature of compassion. This led to us derive the four pillars of compassion which are:

- Awareness of the suffering of another (really noticing/ paying attention)
- Intention to make a difference: ethics, values, sense of self
- Taking action, actively making a difference
- Gently letting go (equanimity).

03

THE SCIENCE OF COMPASSION

From the monastery to the laboratory

Is there an evidence base for compassion? Or is it a deeply philosophical concept with little basis in objective science? Is it possible to see compassion in action within the human brain? We don't have complete answers to these questions, but cutting edge neuroscientific research and brain imaging studies have started to provide intriguing glimpses of the neural circuitry that are likely to be involved in compassion. In the following paragraphs, I present summaries of some recent studies that illustrate the type of research and typical findings from work in this field, utilising both first and third person perspectives.

The first study involves an experiment that has been replicated in a number of ways by different researchers with fairly consistent results. It is called the "empathy for pain" paradigm. One set of typical experiments was conducted at the Wellcome Neuroimaging centre in the United Kingdom. The research investigated what happens in the brains of people when they show empathy with someone else's pain (Klimecki, Ricard and Singer, 2013).

There were two groups of people whose brains were scanned: people actually experiencing painful sensations and a group of people observing someone else experiencing pain. The results showed that when you experience pain yourself, two brain regions called the anterior insula and the anterior cingulate cortex fire up. These regions are associated with the *unpleasantness* aspects of pain.

Now, when you merely observe someone else experiencing pain – with an abstract clue such as the length of an arrow to indicate the intensity of stimulation applied to the other person – the very same neural regions fire up in your brain. The activation of similar brain regions suggests that our emotions are the same whether we observe someone else's pain or experience pain ourselves. These networks are called "empathy for pain" circuits. They fire up regularly in experiments where one person is exposed to another's pain.

This provides a neural clue to the nature of feelings of empathy for someone else's pain: We literally feel the "same", as the same brain circuits are activated in both those who experience pain and observers of others' suffering. When we say, "I feel your pain" or "I know how you feel", this research indicates that our words may quite literally reflect our experiences.

In the second study, researchers in Germany asked a Buddhist monk who was an experienced meditator to take part in an experiment where they scanned his brain. In the first condition, they asked him to immerse himself in sharing the emotional pain of others, and found these very same "empathy for pain" networks firing up. The subjective report of the meditator indicated that engaging in this mind state for about an hour was exhausting and emotionally draining (Klimecki, Ricard and Singer, 2013).

They then asked the meditator to engage in mentally projecting compassion and loving kindness towards others who are suffering. To the researchers' surprise, a different set of brain regions fired up. This involved a complex set of circuits that were different from the empathy for pain network. These included the medial orbitofrontal cortex (the part of the brain at the front of the skull behind the eyes), as well as parts of the brain's reward and affiliation circuits. When asked about the subjective experience of this meditation, the meditator reported a warm positive emotional state with a strong motivation to relieve suffering.

The experimenters also asked the meditator if he wished to follow up his empathy meditation – which led to distress – with a compassion meditation and to the meditator's surprise, he felt the compassionate mental state relieved the distress induced by the empathy meditation.

Although this first person account does not present definitive evidence for the power of compassion to relieve the distress caused by exposure to others' suffering ("empathy for pain"), we are starting to gain some intriguing glimpses into the inner workings of the compassionate mind. Simultaneously, we are also discovering more about the potential of compassion to heal us from the impact of the emotional cost of caring for others.

In an interesting continuation of their work, the researchers then expanded their studies by teaching a group of research participants compassion-based meditation using exercises similar to the ones presented in the *Appendix*. Prior to practising compassion meditation, when they were asked to focus empathically on others' distress, the same empathy for pain neural networks observed previously fired up in the brain, accompanied by subjective feelings of distress.

Following one day's worth of compassion meditation work, their subjective responses to suffering were altogether different. In their cases, the same "compassion networks" as those in the brain of the experienced meditator mentioned above fired up in the scanner – accompanied by similar subjective experiences of positive emotions.

The implications of these preliminary studies of compassion in the brain for staff in care services include the following:

- Empathic responses to others' distress reliably activate different brain regions to compassionate and loving-kindness based responses.

- Empathic concern for the suffering of others can be a distressing experience and a risk factor for burnout. Prolonged activation of the brain's "empathy for pain" circuits can lead to feelings of distress and emotional strain. Feeling overwhelmed in the face of others' suffering, with consequent feelings of depression are classic features of burnout as first formulated by Christina Maslach in the early 1970s (Maslach, 1982).

- It is possible that activation of the brain's compassion circuits can have a restorative function – even in situations where individuals are experiencing empathy-related distress. Care staff cultivating compassion in themselves can therefore employ their compassion focus as a coping resource when faced with their own distressed reactions to others' suffering.

- The last research study reviewed seems to indicate that, under the right conditions, and with practice, the brain's compassion responses can be activated, even in people not initially skilled in meditation.

A scientific model of compassion

Drawing on studies such as the ones cited above, researchers have devised a psychological model of compassion, based on both traditional wisdom and neuroscience research. It is called the ReSource model (Bornemann & Singer, 2013). This model very neatly summarises the psychological factors involved in compassion, but also leads to research hypotheses that scientists can test in the field or in the laboratory in order to advance our understanding of this concept and its implications for individuals and society.

The ReSource model

As we have seen above, neuroscientific research has started to offer a better understanding of the nature of compassion and how compassion affects the brain. The ReSource model starts with taking a renewed look at the definitions of compassion.

I mentioned earlier that one way to define compassion is the awareness of the suffering of others with a strong wish or intention to reduce or ameliorate it. However, traditionally, compassion is also seen as a way of life (Bornemann & Singer, 2013).

If compassion is viewed as a broad orientation to life, or perhaps as a kind of lifestyle choice, then it stands to reason that a compassionate individual will develop and grow a set of attitudes, behaviour, and thought processes that are broadly consistent with their compassion focus. In the language of psychology, a compassionate orientation to life would impact on the following dimensions of psychological functioning (Bornemann & Singer, 2013):

- **Cognitive:** how we think about ourselves and others and which perspectives we assume.

- **Motivational:** our intentions and motivations towards self and others.

- **Socio-affective:** the emotional components of compassion that link with our perspective taking, motivations, or intentions.

In addition, contemplative traditions that focus on compassion as a pervasive orientation to life view compassion as part of our inherent human nature. The preconditions for cultivating compassion, mentioned in the previous chapter, therefore serve to enable our compassionate selves to emerge out of the qualities already present in us.

Drawing together these perspectives with our modern understanding of how the brain functions, the ReSource model formulates the psychology of compassion as a three-dimensional construct, consisting of *presence*, *affect*, and *perspective*.

Presence

Presence is about paying attention to one's own internal states and those of others. Internal states refer to all our thoughts, emotions, sensations, and other mental events such as interoception (body awareness). To be compassionately present, you need to cultivate the skill and discipline involved in stabilising your mind and tolerating the experience of different aspects of yourself in the here and now.

This includes being able to find a quiet internal space, and acceptance or tolerance of unpleasant sensations, thoughts or emotions without judgement. Meditations 1–3 in the *Appendix* can help you get started with cultivating a mental space that allows you to be accepting of your own mental processes, and develop the quietness of mind that will enable you to pay attention in a compassionate way.

Brain regions that are involved in crafting this dimension include the prefrontal cortex, thalamus and parts of the parietal lobes (Bornemann & Singer, 2013).

Affect

The affective dimension refers to opening one's heart to oneself and others, accepting one's own feelings (even if these involve intense discomfort), and developing a strong motivation towards altruism and showing kindness to others. It also involves the capability to generate feelings of warmth and benevolence towards others. Meditations 4 and 5 address this dimension of compassion, including the essential element of compassionate intent towards oneself.

Regions of the brain involved in affiliation and motivation include, for example, the prefrontal cortex and the neuro-endocrine system linked to hormones associated with attachment and affiliation, such as oxytocin and dopamine.

Perspective

This is the cognitive – thinking and imagining – domain of compassion. For true compassion, the individual needs to be able to take an "observational" stance towards their own thinking (metacognition) and develop the ability to take others' perspectives. In addition, there is an element of non-judgement which involves acceptance (of even disturbing or unpleasant aspects of the self/others), and non-attachment or equanimity which is about not needing to hang on to or be needed by the other.

The philosopher Martin Buber draws on these ideas when he talks about developing an "I–Thou" relationship with another (Buber, 1937). Such a relationship involves meeting in a way that honours the humanity of the other without engaging in any of the attachments that can form between people and limit growth and development through need or expectation.

Brain regions concerned include those parts of the prefrontal cortex involved in abstract thinking, sense of self and related functions of the personality, as well as areas at the junctions between the frontal, parietal and temporal lobes which are involved in cross-modal and integrative processing of sensory signals and linking in sense-making to perceptual experiences (Bornemann & Singer, 2013).

For reflection...

- What is your experience of stress and burnout? Do you think the link between empathic concern and emotional distress demonstrated in laboratory settings is also valid in practice in your service? If so, what are your views on the findings mentioned above related to compassion-focused meditation as a way to manage empathic distress?

- The ReSource model provides a neuropsychological foundation for understanding compassion. Considering the paragraphs on presence, affect, and perspective, how do these dimensions link with the four pillars of compassion we derived from contemplative traditions? These were:
  - awareness of suffering
  - intention (to make a difference)
  - compassionate action
  - equanimity.

04

MINDFULNESS AND COMPASSION

What I'm looking for is not out there, it is in me.

– Helen Keller

Mindfulness, just like compassionate care, has become a very popular concept lately. However, I believe that developing certain mindfulness skills is a critical prerequisite to a mature, compassionate approach to delivering care. Becoming mindful is therefore both one of the pre-conditions for cultivating compassion in oneself, and also a key part of the first pillar of compassion, namely, really paying attention to suffering. In this chapter, I provide a brief overview of mindfulness with specific reference to the relevance of the concept to compassionate care, the focus of this book. Readers who wish to explore the field of mindfulness further can consult the many excellent books and websites available on the topic for more information.

Defining mindfulness

Mindfulness as a concept has its origins in Buddhist philosophy and practice. In recent decades the concept has been adopted by many in the West and adapted into a powerful set of practices that have applications across a range of disciplines, including clinical and occupational psychology. Academic research into mindfulness-based therapeutic approaches have shown very promising results for a number of therapies (Hayes, 2004; Kabat-Zinn, 1982; Teasdale, Segal & Williams, 1995).

To be mindful can be defined as experiencing a present-centred awareness of one's mental processes with non-judgemental acceptance (Kabat-Zinn, 1994).

There are a few key points to note about this definition. Being mindful involves, first of all, paying attention. Awareness of one's own processes – thoughts, feelings, and sensations that arise from within the body as the flow of consciousness proceeds from moment to moment. This links in with the first pillar of compassion mentioned in a previous chapter – awareness of, or paying attention to suffering in ourselves and others. However, the mindful approach also links with the fourth pillar of compassion, equanimity. Being mindful involves acceptance and letting go of thoughts, sensations, memories and emotions.

Mindful awareness involves understanding and accepting that life consists of a sequence of moments. Each one is unique in the opportunities it brings, each one is filled with sensations, thoughts and feelings. Each one is fleeting and never to be repeated. Mindful acceptance means that we do not deny the impact of our experiences on us, but that we experience what *is* with an awareness of its true nature: thoughts are just thoughts, images are images that arise in our minds, memories are constructed from stored fragments and associations preserved in our neural circuitry. Our concerns, worries, and distress arise from within and belong to us in that sense. We suffer needlessly when we view our thoughts and imaginings as equivalent to reality itself.

Mindfulness does not always come naturally to us. We are prone to experience our "mental chatter" as reality (Rao, 2015). We also often do one thing, while thinking another and therefore never really pay attention to the moment at hand (Gilbert, 2010). Opting out of our natural inclination to immerse ourselves in our own mental experiences and view these as reality itself, takes disciplined practice.

There are many ways to do this, and you might find some of the meditations offered in the *Appendix* helpful to develop your own mindfulness practice. But how about starting straight away with a very simple exercise. Just close your eyes for a moment and focus on the sensory world around you. What can you hear? What do you feel? Are you warm or cold? Try to spend about half a minute doing this. Then focus on the sensations that arise from within your body, and the stream of consciousness in your mind: What are you thinking or imagining? Are you remembering, planning, rehearsing conversations, worrying, or maybe imagining a scene or a situation? Try to spend a minute or two in self-observation.

Mindfulness practice starts with spending quiet time regularly, just crafting your awareness of your own internal processes with the kind of equanimity mentioned earlier: accept and let go, realising that in the next moment there is space for something different or something new to arise.

Mindfulness practice can nurture compassion

The research cited in the previous chapter provided preliminary findings suggesting that neural networks associated with compassion and positive emotions can be strengthened by practising compassion meditation techniques. Although it has not yet been established that this kind of meditation can also increase individuals' compassionate actions, these findings do present a promising avenue for those wishing to nurture and cultivate their compassionate selves.

The next chapter presents a more detailed "road map" for compassionate practice. The contribution that developing your mindfulness can make towards this is, however, very important. We shall see later that compassion is a dynamic process that flows from an inward to an outward focus. Mindfulness practices can help us channel our compassion in accordance with this dynamic flow, and assist us in nurturing and developing compassionate awareness and intent, two of the four pillars of compassion.

As an illustration of one mindfulness-based compassion exercise, try the following: Think of someone for whose kindness or help you feel grateful. While you relax your body and close your eyes, bring this person to mind and radiate your good wishes and gratitude to them. You might wish to repeat a phrase to yourself that expresses your wish for this person, such as, "May you be well and happy". Doing this for a few minutes might put you in touch with your own gratitude towards this specific individual, but perhaps also with feelings of gratitude in general. Carefully observe your own mindset once you have completed this exercise. Do you notice any differences between the way you approached your day before and after completing this task?

Mindfulness involves two key cognitive processes that affect individuals' experience of their own mental processes: First of all, mindfulness, as defined earlier, consists of an awareness of our mental processes in the present. In mindfulness practices, such as the meditations in the *Appendix*, this often involves actively focusing our awareness on bodily sensations, thoughts, sensory experiences, and so forth. This process of active focusing soon becomes automated and less effortful with practice. Awareness of our own processes forms the foundation for really noticing others in all their humanity. And so actively focusing inwards teaches us how to pay attention – firstly to ourselves and later on to others. This process paves the way for internalising the first pillar of compassion; really paying attention both to the suffering self and the suffering of others.

The second important cognitive component of mindfulness involves the awareness and acceptance of mental processes for what they are: suffering lies in embracing distressing emotions, worries and thoughts as our reality, rather than "thinking about" them as "just" worries, thoughts or feelings (i.e., mental processes arising in the brain, and not objectively true or real). Mindfulness practices help us to develop a different meta-cognitive perspective – that of dispassionate observers of our own thought processes. This links in with the "perspective" domain of the ReSource model of compassion mentioned earlier (Bornemann & Singer, 2013). We can therefore experience our thoughts with full awareness, and yet not be subject to them.

The neuroscientific research reviewed earlier indicates that our brains are wired for compassion. Contemplative approaches reflect this by believing that compassion grows from within our humanity, given the right preconditions. Mindfulness is one such precondition and important because mindful awareness does not come naturally to us. We need to spend time training our minds in these skills.

The meta-cognitive perspective of mindful awareness, as well as the ability to truly pay attention to our own minds and experiences, are precursors to the pillars of compassion. Living life mindfully can enable us to free our mental focus from a preoccupation with our own mental lives to becoming more open to the world around us and therefore to really noticing the suffering of others with compassionate intent.

For reflection...

In this chapter we briefly considered mindfulness as a precondition for some of the pillars of compassion. I also mentioned the power of regular and disciplined practice to enable mindfulness skills to become internalised and automated. What might be the obstacles for you to developing mindful self-awareness? (Starting out on such a journey, you would probably need to focus on exercises such as the simple mindfulness meditation on sensory and thought awareness given earlier, or use some of the exercises from the *Appendix* on a regular basis.)

Can you think of ways in which you can overcome these obstacles?

Mindfulness approaches have also become quite frequently used in health care settings to help people deal with stress, depression, and anxiety. How do you think mindfulness can contribute to mental wellbeing? I had promising results with brief mindfulness sessions (15 minutes each) run once a week for staff in a large mental health team, in terms of participants reporting a positive impact on their level of work stress. Can you think of possible applications to your work setting?

05
A ROADMAP FOR COMPASSIONATE PRACTICE

Only when we know our own darkness well can we be present with the darkness of others. Compassion becomes real when we recognize our shared humanity.

— Pema Chödrön

Growing your compassion

I mentioned the idea of cultivating compassion earlier on. This section describes a set of practices that are designed to help you do just this (Jinananda, 2012). Before I present these in detail, here is just a word on some important points related to the cultivation of compassion that are drawn from contemplative traditions mentioned throughout the earlier chapters.

We have seen that cultivation involves setting in place those conditions necessary for growth to occur. A seed will only germinate if the conditions are right, but once those preconditions are in place, the young seedling is able to grow and even flourish. In the previous chapter, we discussed developing mindfulness as one such precondition for compassion to grow. A further precondition – especially if we want our compassionate selves to become stronger and flourish – is that, paradoxically, we need to develop compassion for ourselves.

By cultivating self-compassion, we turn towards our own suffering and face our own pain. We learn to accept the whole of ourselves with equanimity. We develop awareness of how our own mental processes are contributing to our suffering by holding us back and taking our focus away from each moment with all its potential. Understanding, acceptance, and awareness of our suffering helps us to be less preoccupied with our own issues and frees us to pay attention to the pain of others.

The second important perspective is that the compassionate part of human nature is vulnerable and will only emerge and thrive under the right conditions, including the absence of the enemies of compassion, as described previously. Especially relevant to compassionate practice are the many subtle ways in which helpers can "hang on" to those they support. Fundamental assumptions about service users perhaps being helpless, infantile, incompetent, abandoned and in need of rescue, can all feed into our own need to be needed. Even "good practice" based on these motivations can at best be "empathic" – leading to "empathy for pain" circuits activating regularly and increasing the risk of burnout.

Compassionate practice is fundamentally based on the notion that human beings contain within them both the seeds of suffering and those of their own healing. The role of the helper can be viewed as supporting another human being to engage with the healing force within and, once the healing process has progressed sufficiently, to enable the person to proceed on his or her own journey (equanimity). Compassionate practice aims to let go, while, more often than we would like to admit, empathic helping is really about holding on, strengthening our own sense of self-worth, or binding others to ourselves with bonds of gratitude or obligation.

The steps outlined below offer but one path towards developing compassion. This particular path may not be for you, in which case, you might have to engage with a different path or even develop your own. More common, I believe, might be the experience of finding some use in these ideas, with the rest coming from within. What is most important, though, is that you respond to your own intention to become more compassionate by engaging with practices that will enable you to turn this intention into action.

Don't be mistaken, however. This process is deceptively difficult to realise. The only place it can emanate from is within you, before your compassion can radiate outwards. Therefore, the most potent obstacles are likely to be those within yourself. If you are able to persist and overcome these, you will reap a wide range of benefits, including new ways of thinking, doing, and being that will reflect a more accepting stance towards yourself and others.

What does compassionate intent mean?

The idea of cultivating an intention needs to be clarified too. When you feel hungry and you make yourself a sandwich, the mental processes involved in changing what you are doing, going to the kitchen, taking out the bread, and so forth, represent the actions you take in response to your intention. Prior to acting on your intention, you became aware of something – the feeling of hunger and perhaps some imagery related to what would satisfy your need. Your intention contained both an awareness of your need or want, and a volitional component – what you want to do to enact the intention. Another example – with a longer-term impact – might be saving up for a holiday. The overriding intention might be to realise the opportunity for a dream vacation. On a weekly basis you might act on this intention by saving some of your income until, many weeks or months later, you have enough money to act directly on your intention and book your holiday.

When we mention intentions towards self or others in the section below, these twin components both apply: When you say, "May I be well and healthy" that sentence serves as more than a lovely sentiment to repeat often as part of an internal dialogue. For it to qualify as an intention, it needs to have those very same two components of emotional awareness and volitional activation that made you get up from where you were when you felt hungry, and go into the kitchen to make a sandwich. The same principles apply whether the intention is expressed towards friend or foe, towards humanity in general, or even the planet we inhabit. This is not an easy idea to grasp and often quite a difficult concept to put into practice. Yet, if you fully intend compassion towards yourself, others, or humanity as a whole, this can be both liberating and life changing. And you will become able to touch the lives of others in a quite different way.

Developing a compassionate mind

Perhaps convinced of the benefits of cultivating compassion in yourself, you may now legitimately ask, how do I realise this compassionate way of living on a day-to-day basis? As we have seen, this might involve setting in place the right preconditions for your inherent compassion to emerge, and working on developing compassionate intent with persistence and discipline.

Placing compassionate thoughts and behaviours at the

centre of your values, and actively practising compassionate actions in every area of your life, will allow the compassionate parts of yourself to emerge and flourish. Yet every seed needs nutrients in order to grow and develop into a thriving, mature plant.

In order to germinate and grow your compassion, you will need to develop compassion-enhancing practices in your life and show compassionate intent in your actions. Traditional approaches to contemplation and meditation have delineated a path that you could follow in your daily practice in order to "till the soil" for your compassionate self.

For each of these steps, you may find it helpful to spend some time each day reflecting on the theme represented in that stage of the journey towards true compassion. Compassion-focused meditation practices, such as the seven meditations offered in the *Appendix*, will also help you to do this. But your meditation and reflection need to be augmented by the intelligent kindness dimension of compassion. In other words, not only do you need to develop the mental discipline through daily practice, but you also need to strengthen your intention through compassionate action.

Step 1: Compassion towards the self

Self-compassion involves both compassionate intent and compassionate action towards the self. Compassionate intent towards oneself may be expressed in the phrases, "May I be well", "May I be happy" (Jinananda, 2012). These words are labels used to express something more than just a nice sentiment or a mantra. They are designed to become the focus of your mental energy, a genuine wish for yourself.

Happiness, you might think, is what everyone wants. And that may be true, but, in many cases, a genuine wish for oneself to be happy may be absent, as many people do not truly believe that they are worthy of happiness. Previous bad experiences or past trauma may have resulted in psychological wounds such as low self-esteem or fundamental beliefs that reflect a sense of unworthiness or even a fear of happiness or wellness. Therapists all too often hear the sentiment expressed that "when something good happens, I just wait for the inevitable disaster to follow."

Self-compassion is therefore underpinned by an acceptance of even the darkest parts of oneself and the fundamental belief that "I am worthy" of being well, happy, fortunate, and so forth (even if I have a side to me that is frightening and dark). For many, just getting to a place where they feel able to be self-compassionate is consequently a journey of growth and development in and of itself.

One of the key early stages in this journey is the ability to spend some quiet time with one's own thoughts. How easy is this for you to do? For some, just being alone and quiet is a serious challenge. All too often, hidden behind our busy lives, lies a fundamental fear of being alone or of being quiet with our own thoughts. Practising the first meditation given in the *Appendix* may be one way to find quiet inner space, but even this practice may be quite difficult to start with. Another way to get started might be to find somewhere in nature where you can spend some time alone. Go for a walk on the beach on your own, with no distractions, or go and sit on a park bench for a few minutes on your own. The key to using these activities as starting points for developing internal quiet space, is that you need to practise focusing your attention away from thinking, ruminating, worrying and so forth, and instead focus your awareness on your senses: what do you see, hear, or feel around you?

Of course, the end result of true compassionate intent towards oneself is compassionate action towards oneself. This could involve actively accepting the least liked parts of yourself, taking care of yourself, or refraining from unbalanced, self-damaging behaviour.

A key enemy of self-compassion is self-deprecation. How often do you negatively judge yourself? How frequently do you say to yourself, "I am so stupid" or "I am a terrible person"? One key step towards cultivating self-compassion is simply to stop yourself doing this. Put an end to self-deprecating internal verbalisations by catching yourself out when you do this, and refraining from verbalising those self-judging words any further. (Even if you still feel you believe or even deserve the self-criticism, simply by refraining from verbalising it, you are taking a small step towards healing. The more you eliminate those self-deprecating narratives from your internal dialogue, the less you reinforce your own self-loathing.)

Self-compassion in the contemplative traditions involves three elements: self-kindness, mindfulness, and a sense of common humanity (Neff & Germer, 2013). Self-kindness is very much about those mental and practical acts of self-care and self-acceptance described above. Mindfulness, in this context, is a non-judgemental acceptance of oneself and one's internal reality in the present moment. This is a little like the idea of "presence" in the ReSource model described above, except that one is fully present within one's own reality.

This type of mindfulness is really much harder in practice than might be apparent at first. Self-directed mindfulness involves crafting the ability to stay with your own internal turmoil, accepting the distressing and darker sides of your own nature without adding self-judgement into the mix.

Self-acceptance in this context is very different from an unquestioning self-indulgence that can lead to a destructive degree of arrogance and narcissism. Self-compassion at its best leads to awareness and acceptance of one's own weaknesses, flaws, and limitations – and consequently to humility. Self-compassion is also an acknowledgement of one's own need for compassion. This is the opposite of responding with defensive reactions such as denial, or the deep sense of shame that comes from a catastrophic reaction to one's own shortcomings.

The third dimension of self-compassion is a natural product of the other two, namely, a renewed sense of your own humanity in the context of the common humanity of us all: an "I–Thou encounter" with the human race (Buber, 1937). Just as I am human and carry with me my private as well as public joys and sorrows, so it is with us all. It is inevitable that when we take a compassionate stance towards our internal worlds, we start to look at the world outside with new, more compassionate eyes.

That all sounds fine, but what good does it do? Is self-compassion not just an inch away from narcissism? Could accepting the darker side of my nature not lead straight to an arrogant denial of the need for humility, despite all the nice sentiments expressed above? What is the evidence for the "added value" of self-compassion for people in general and specifically for practitioners of health and social care?

There are research studies that have shown a whole host of benefits associated with high self-compassion (Neff & Germer, 2013). For example, individuals with high self-compassion are less destructively critical of themselves and others. They are less prone to depression and anxiety, and more capable of dealing with stress. They are more able to show kindness and compassion towards others. In both close (intimate partner) and caring (professional) relationships, individuals high in self-compassion are viewed more positively and are perceived by others as more compassionate. The studies reviewed by Neff and Germer (2013) therefore show that in both their personal and professional lives individuals high in self-compassion reap benefits and that high self-compassion may be a determinant of better mental health. Psychologists have not been slow to apply these findings to therapeutic treatments for mental health problems and enhancing wellbeing, one example being the compassion-focused therapy developed by Paul Gilbert (2010).

When we cultivate compassion in our lives, it stands to reason that we are likely to develop a range of virtues and coping skills that emerge from our compassionate orientation to self and others. The psychologist Paul Gilbert (2010) lists some of these. Here I restate them in the form of "I" statements which link in with the ideas about self-compassion that are discussed in the text.

Manifesto for self-compassion

I am deeply committed to myself; I desire to cope with and relieve my own suffering. I take joy in my happiness.

I am not overwhelmed by my own pain and remain present, enduring my distress with equanimity.

I have developed the wisdom to live in the moment. I am just here where I am in the present moment, doing my best to deal with my struggles.

I am warm and caring; I am open to both myself and others and committed to gentleness, caring and openness to experience.

I am not judgemental or critical; my response is acceptance, and commitment to the relief of my own and others' struggles.

Step 2: Compassion towards a "good friend"

The second step along the journey towards cultivating your own compassion is to develop compassionate intent towards a good friend. Most people find this quite easy, provided they can bring to mind someone who they care about, who has shown them a kindness, or who is a good friend.

As in the previous step, compassionate intent grows through practice, through both action and mental focus: find a period of time each day where you focus your mental attention on your friend and your intention for their happiness, health and wellbeing.

There is a temptation for many of us to spend time developing this compassion towards another at the expense of self-compassion, but, as we have seen above, people who are high in self-compassion are also experienced as more compassionate by others. This research finding emphasises the importance of maintaining self-compassion at all stages of the journey towards a compassionate life.

Step 3: Compassion towards a neutral person

One step beyond compassion towards oneself and compassion towards a good friend is developing compassionate intent towards a specific, but neutral person. Preferably this would be someone you have had some dealings with, but perhaps not someone who is close to you. The neutral person could be the person who cleans your windows, collects your household waste, or perhaps someone who you see regularly on your commute, but do not know. Compassionate intent towards a neutral person really involves stepping out of our normal mode of measuring people and judging them. Setting aside our own projections, expectations, and prejudices, we can meet them as fellow human beings at the junction of our common humanities.

Moving the focus of your compassionate intent from a friend to a relative stranger takes you one step beyond the knowns of your life towards the unknown. Yet there is an important benefit in this step for further mastery of the earlier steps too, as it may be easier to feel compassion with equanimity for a stranger than for either a friend or for oneself. Focusing our attention on compassion for a neutral person can therefore teach us valuable lessons about letting go of potentially unhelpful emotional bonds that may present our own emotional projections and needs, rather than true compassionate intent.

Step 4: Compassion for an enemy

One of the key dimensions of self-compassion is the sense of being part of a common, shared humanity with all other human beings on this planet. As humans we share a set of biological functions, we dream, we strive, and we have an extraordinary capacity to learn and adapt. A key part of our humanness is that we can feel and show compassion, kindness, and mercy to others.

Just as self-compassion involves acceptance of even the shadows in our own personalities, so compassion for other human beings involves the challenge of developing compassionate intent towards those who do not wish us well – our "enemies". This is a strong imperative in many world religions and spiritual traditions. Compassion for the enemy is, for many, a mark of spiritual growth and maturity. Cultivating this very difficult intention is, however, a precondition for developing universal compassion, which is all-inclusive.

The "enemy" here should be taken to mean a wide range of people who annoy, irritate, and even hate us. Your enemy is the one who cannot stand you and the one who you cannot abide. It's the workplace bully and the annoying neighbour, but it can also be those who bring you down through their attitudes, jealousy, or their machinations to sabotage your journey in any aspect of your life.

The compassionate way of life is therefore also a way of life that does not bear grudges, where injuries are forgiven, and where others' short-sighted, small-minded thoughts and actions are met with kindness, forgiveness, and making a choice against vengeance in all its forms.

Perhaps of all the aspects of compassionate living, this represents the biggest ask. However, it also frees the mind from negative energy and preoccupation that come with dwelling on insults, slights, injustices and gossip. The compassionate mind that is able to exhibit compassion, even for an enemy, is therefore a mind that is free: free to pay attention, free to notice the suffering of others, and free to care.

Step 5: Universal compassion

Cultivating compassion started with looking inward, with mindful, non-judgemental acceptance of oneself, self-kindness, and a sense of sharing in a common humanity. The paradox of compassion is that looking inward must inevitably lead to the focus of compassion moving outward. Beyond the self there is the friend, the neutral person, the enemy, humanity, all living things, and then the universe itself. This is the culmination of the compassionate way of life.

Universal compassion, like all compassion, involves more than just focusing compassionate intent. It also implies compassionate action. Universal compassion manifests in our lifestyle choices: what we eat, where we get our energy from, how we treat nature in all its forms. Compassionate living is therefore a pervasive choice that affects our inner lives, our actions towards others, and the way we live: the inward focus that starts with self-compassion, where the seed of compassion germinates, grows into a tree with branches that reach out towards others, the whole of humanity, the planet we call home, and beyond.

Developing compassionate action

The previous section mentioned the inextricable link between an internal compassion focus and our overt behaviour. This is true for both our lives outside of work and the ways in which we perform our duties at work. The compassionate way involves making an effort to notice what it is like for someone to need our services and how they might experience us.

Really noticing means taking the time to have a look at what we do and how we do it. What is it like for someone to phone us up, to come into our waiting room, to receive the letters we write to them? How does it feel to receive a service from us and what does the care pathway feel like from the perspective of the person who uses the service? Are we so "professional" that we are no longer friendly and welcoming? Do we behave towards the recipients of our services in ways that make them feel that we are compassionate towards them, or do we make them feel judged, incapable, or resented for needing us?

Compassionate action, as one definition referred to earlier makes clear, involves intelligent kindness. This hints at both a kind way of being with people, and the sophisticated theoretical and practical knowledge and skills needed to deliver health and social care in the 21st century. Yet how one would achieve this in teams and organisations remains a challenge which we turn to in the next chapter.

For reflection...

In this chapter we discussed a number of steps in the journey towards a compassionate self. Which of these do you feel might be most challenging for you? How do you think being truly self-compassionate would make a difference to practitioners in your type of work?

In the next chapter, we discuss developing compassionate services and teams. Take a few minutes to review the material in this chapter that you think might have practical implications for that process.

INTERLUDE
THE FLOW OF COMPASSION

We have seen that compassion, once we start to cultivate it in our lives, permeates through our thought processes, attitudes, and eventually our actions as well. The dynamics of compassion are as important as the characteristics of compassion, which has been the predominant topic of this book so far. However, in the previous chapters we did come across intriguing glimpses as to the direction in which compassion flows. We have seen that cultivating compassion starts with focusing on self-compassion, before proceeding to compassion for a friend, a neutral person, an enemy, and the world. Compassion starts with an inward flow, but cannot remain confined within an inward-bound trajectory. Once compassion starts to guide our focus, it inevitably requires an ever-increasing radius of influence. Inward focused compassion, once established, transforms into a wave of outward flowing pulses of compassionate awareness, intent, and action, taking our compassion out of our personal spaces to the world beyond the horizon.

Compassion first moves inwards (self-compassion) and then ever outwards into the world, like the widening ripples of a pebble falling into a pond.

06

DEVELOPING COMPASSIONATE TEAMS, SERVICES AND ORGANISATIONS

I alone cannot change the world, but I can cast a
stone across the water to create many ripples.

— Mother Teresa

In the first five chapters of this book, I shared with you some thoughts on the journey to becoming a more compassionate person and practitioner. Along the way, we considered the nature of compassion, the ways in which we can cultivate a more compassionate orientation to life and work, and also thought about the role of mindfulness in nurturing compassion, and the emerging scientific evidence on the power of compassion to refresh the mind and heal the wounds of "empathic distress".

Developing a more compassionate self turned out to be a journey requiring disciplined practice and self-acceptance. In the text and in the *Appendix*, I offer various exercises you can use to help you along the way. As a practitioner, however, the question that may be close to your heart at this stage is "How can we translate the principles we have learned into practice in the context of teams, services, and organisations?" In this closing chapter, I offer some initial thoughts on how systems of care can become more compassion-focused.

Cultivating compassion within systems

Returning to the agricultural metaphor we discussed earlier, the first step in enhancing the compassion-focus of your team, service, or organisation is to set in place the right preconditions for the inherent compassion of the people in the system to emerge and thrive. Nurturing compassion within different parts of a system might involve different approaches for different teams, but the broad principles are valid across all teams and all systems.

Cultivate awareness

This involves developing ways of working that encourage *really noticing* the suffering of service users. Paying attention to what is happening for the people who use your service may involve looking beyond the formal reasons for their referral. Someone who is homeless may, in addition to a need for shelter, also carry with them the uncertainty of rootlessness (a sense of not belonging), a sense of loss of place or identity, and perhaps even deep wounds caused by displacement. Someone with a mental health problem may bring into the service with them their fear of loss of their mental integrity, or the traumas of relationship loss and loneliness. Each person has a story that stretches beyond the questions on your intake form. Do you truly wish to understand their pain? Do you see a person or a patient, an individual, or a "case"? Do you know? Do you ask?

Develop compassionate intent

In cash-strapped, hard-pressed services, it is easy to look for reasons to decline, discharge, or minimise what is offered. I am not arguing for expansive, clingy services that try to comprehensively deliver it all. That is simply not viable. But I believe, from experience, that the narratives we engage in about people who use our services are very closely linked to how we treat them and what we offer.

How does your team talk about the people you work with? Listen to the language in meetings and the narratives used in reports, supervision, and informal conversations. Ask yourself if that reflects compassionate intent. (We defined compassionate intent previously as the ardent wish to make a difference and alleviate suffering combined with the motivation to take action – are we really interested in taking action to alleviate distress, or would we rather this was someone else's problem?)

Paying attention to someone's suffering as individual practitioners or as teams or services, does not invariably mean more work or utilising more resources, but it does mean that we look closely at the suffering and need of the person in front of us, and find out what it is that would really make a difference to them. Often it is not the resource-intensive interventions we might fear, but something much more modest. The alleviation of the other's suffering may even fall within the remit of another service. However, compassionate action may involve just going that extra distance to make sure the person is able to access the help they need, perhaps through spending a few minutes writing a letter or making a phone call on their behalf. More often though, compassion shows through when we just listen or, more subtly, in the tone of voice we use, or the respect with which we address people.

Take compassionate action

Do our services enable staff to take compassionate action? Do we encourage practitioners to show curiosity and get to know the person in front of them to the degree that they could gain a sense of the individual's suffering and need? (How one would go about doing this will differ from service to service.) This is also where the enemies of compassion come into play: time pressure and institutional defences counteract staff members' inherent compassionate focus. Compassionate teams develop their awareness *as a team* and this takes time together. When we allow time pressure to deny us the opportunity to meet together to think and reflect on how we can cultivate compassion in our service, we are giving in to one of the most potent enemies of compassion in systems and organisations. Note too how often we claim time pressure or organisational priorities as problems preventing us from being compassionate, as if these difficulties are imposed on us from beyond our own spheres of influence. Perhaps we should challenge ourselves to examine how often in our own services these pressures are, in fact, very powerful distancing defences, preventing us from looking closer and really noticing the suffering of others, protecting us from the impact on ourselves of the distress and vulnerability we encounter.

Letting go

As was mentioned earlier, equanimity is the important (fourth) pillar of compassion. How are you and your team with gently letting go? Does your understanding of what you offer people who use your services include clarity about when they might be able to go on their disparate ways without your help? A compassionate service notices need *and* vulnerability, but balances that awareness with support and interventions that build competence, rather than interventions that keep people dependent.

Equanimity, in this context, differs from pressure to discharge, as it draws on a genuine desire to enable someone to move forward on their journey, rather than a service focus on throughput. A further, more subtle enemy of compassion in services is the temptation to discharge people when they get "better", thus providing an incentive to stay unwell.

Compassionate teams acknowledge the human bonds that form between service users and staff. These relationships frequently carry more meaning to the human beings involved than the formal roles taken by staff members may imply. Endings, just like beginnings, can be traumatic, and have their own dynamics. A compassionate ending, in this context, might have been carefully planned and thoughtfully discussed long before the date of discharge. The interpersonal meaning of the relationship and ways of saying goodbye should be openly approached and worked through, so that both practitioner and service user can move on with their journeys.

The main point of the above paragraphs is that compassion in services affects all aspects of the work: the systems and procedures we put in place, the way we deliver services, management of relationships, and even the ways we approach discharge require careful consideration. From a service planning perspective, cultivating compassion requires attention to the conditions that would nurture and enable compassion to thrive, and also the difficult task of working towards eliminating the enemies of compassion (such as a high degree of time pressure or pressure to achieve throughput) as far as possible. The key step for those readers who wish to start making a difference is to craft, within teams, the capability to continually *pay attention* to these factors.

Compassion flows from inside to outside

Previously we considered the ways in which compassion flows through our lives, from the inside to the outside. The flow of compassion in organisations and teams operates in the same way. Teams that are able to look inward and show true compassion to themselves as teams, will find that, as their self-compassion grows, the flow of compassion will start to expand in focus beyond themselves, towards service users, other parts of their own organisation, and partner organisations.

Self-compassion in a team context might involve focusing on developing more compassionate ways of dealing with one another, really noticing the "suffering" and job stress within the team, and perhaps responding by showing each other kindness. This may involve doing things such as the following:

- Making time to think about compassion within their service.
- Supporting each other through regular time for joint reflective practice.
- Developing a team-based compassion meditation practice.
- Setting in place a "buddy system" relating to the personal impact of work and work–life balance.
- Creating opportunities for the team to learn together.

Compassion percolates through the system

Compassion, once it has started to grow within a system, tends to spread and percolate outwards. As we show compassion to others within the systems we engage with, they in turn might respond with more compassion towards us and those they come into contact with. Our brains are wired to respond to compassion, kindness and altruism (Gilbert, 2010). Therefore, once compassion gains a foothold in your team, or service, the compassion circuits in ever more people will become engaged and, at some point, the ripples will start and compassion will spread.

The path compassion might take through a system, is perhaps unpredictable, but like the mustard seed parable referred to back in *Chapter 1*, what starts off very modestly can grow to become a powerful and influential force for good. Our tasks in this process are twofold: firstly, each one of us could choose to develop and enhance our own compassion, and secondly, within the systems we operate in, each one of us can do all we can to nurture compassion and combat its enemies within our respective spheres of influence. So, if your sphere of influence is relatively limited, you may enhance the compassion focus of your team by being an exemplar of a compassionate practitioner. You could share with your colleagues your ideas and feedback on ways your service could be more compassionate, and you could show compassion to colleagues. If, on the other hand, your sphere of influence is more encompassing, you might be able to influence policy decisions, set in place procedures that facilitate the compassion focus of practitioners, or even ensure that the commissioning of services is done in such a way that compassion, once it takes hold, can thrive.

For reflection...

• One of the underlying assumptions in this chapter is my belief that compassion is an inherent part of human nature that will grow and thrive once the necessary preconditions are in place. On the other hand, compassion is also vulnerable to its enemies, which, in services, might include time pressure and the need to hold on to people who are kept dependent, or a pressure to discharge and achieve a high throughput. I also state that compassion, once able to thrive in one part of a system will, by its nature, percolate through the rest of it, provided the right preconditions are in place. Do you agree or disagree with this? Do you perhaps believe this is an idealistic point of view, not borne out in reality as you see it? If so, what do you believe needs to happen to cultivate compassion in your organisation and enable it to thrive across teams and services?

- Finally, map out your sphere of influence in your role. You can do this by listing those activities, tasks, and meetings you are a part of, or can influence. Which decisions are you empowered to make and how can you influence the way in which work is done in your service or organisation? Now think of the pillars of compassion as listed previously:

  1. Awareness of the suffering of another (really noticing/ paying attention)
  2. Intention to make a difference: ethics, values, sense of self
  3. Taking action, actively making a difference
  4. Gently letting go (equanimity).

How can you affect the ways in which these four aspects of compassion manifest themselves in your organisation through your sphere of influence? What can you do to minimise the impact of organisational enemies of compassion, such as time pressure, and bureaucratic intrusions on the ability of teams and services to show more compassion? How can you promote and cultivate self-compassion at team, service or organisational level?

APPENDIX
MEDITATIONS TO DEVELOP YOUR COMPASSION

Below you will find instructions for seven meditations that are designed to help you set in place the mental practices that form the bedrock for cultivating your compassionate mind. On paper, these might seem quite simple and straightforward – you might even question whether these simple meditations can make any difference at all to your professional practice or your life. Such questions are quite legitimate. The literature on mindfulness and compassionate practice is full of ideas, methods, and techniques that are marketed as panaceas for the stresses of modern life. Perhaps a substantial proportion of these are not helpful to everyone who tries them. Some of these techniques might even appear so "basic" that – on face value – we would simply not believe that they could help us transform ourselves. But look again. These practices may appear simple, yet represent exactly those things we normally tend *not* to do. For example, completing a task mindfully involves really paying attention to what we do, feel and think, and the sensations we experience in the process. This trains our attentional focus on the here and now. However, this type of enhanced focus is exactly the opposite of our usual rushed ways when, as we mentioned in *Chapter 4*, we do one thing and think another (Gilbert, 2010).

I would therefore challenge you to have a go and try some of these – you may find that they are much harder than they appear, but also more powerful tools for change than you might have thought at first. If you do find it difficult, don't despair. Keep on trying. Even your difficulties with these meditations are legitimate mental experiences, worthy of contemplation and tolerating, while you embrace your intent to become more compassionate by not giving up.

From experience, I anticipate that achieving mental quietness, a key component to many of the meditations that follow, may present a particular difficulty for many readers. Remember that during the last few centuries, our brains have become much busier than ever before, in keeping with our information-rich, hyper-connected contemporary lives.

Here are some general tips and ideas that might encourage you to keep up your practice:

Make time to not "do" anything. Compassionate practice starts with planning in a few minutes, maybe 10–15 per day at first, just to *be*. This could be the time you spend on the exercises below, but it needn't be. You need time for contemplation – even if only to allow the many trains of thought going round your mind all at once to reach their destinations, before the next set of thoughts start off on their frantic journeys.

Develop discipline. Many of the discourses about compassion and mindfulness meditation I have come across tend to focus on what I would call the "warm fuzzy" or "quick fix" elements. Mindfulness is painted as a wonderful panacea that will solve all your problems, and turn you into a worry-free individual in no time at all. However, what always strikes me is that a large proportion of those prominent individuals in the mindfulness movement who appear to be able to speak and write most authoritatively on this topic have chosen monastic lives. Why is that? Monastic life in all the great spiritual and religious traditions involves a very high level of self-denial, structure, and self-discipline.

Compassion does not just involve a warm feeling of acceptance towards self and others. True compassion involves both a journey of development predicated on engaging in practices that require high levels of self-discipline, and also compassionate action. Neither of these comes easily; both involve a degree of self-denial and risk-taking. Compassion in its true sense cannot stay inside our minds; it leaks out into our worlds, affecting relationships, activities, and how we live.

Compassion is both a way of being and a "practice". A little here and there, or perhaps even a lot every now and then will not change your life or your practice, even though "part-time" engagement with compassionate practices might lead to good feelings and other positive outcomes, but those will not be sustained in the long run without regular practice and daily commitment.

Commit to the journey: the first time you try one of the exercises below, you may struggle. That is to be expected. Some months later, and you may have outgrown *all* of the exercises below, and be well on your way to developing new compassionate practices and meditations of your own.

The three core components of compassion in the ReSource model discussed in *Chapter 3* – namely, presence, affect and perspective – also include some challenges to our maturation and natural human tendency to worry and cling. We need to learn to pay attention to and "stay with" those very parts of ourselves and others we may intensely dislike; we may have to learn new ways of perceiving injustice; we may need to find new ways of behaving that are consistent with compassionate intent which, as was explained above, is much more than good feelings towards self and others. We might also need to learn to give up some of our most cherished notions, perhaps even about the ways in which we work. For people in the helping professions, for instance, the near enemies of compassion and loving kindness, pity and attachment, are sometimes particularly difficult to acknowledge in ourselves, and even more difficult to shed.

Stay with the flow: compassion always develops from an inward focus to an outward focus. The exercises below, even if done faithfully, will not take you all the way to being a mature, compassionate practitioner. Self-compassion by its nature radiates outwards. This will necessitate that you think about your own professional practice, that of your team, and that of your organisation as a whole. So if you want to cultivate compassion in yourself, be prepared for the time when you will ardently wish for that compassion to spread to your team, service, or organisation.

Seven compassion-building mindfulness meditations

The exercises below have been adapted from many different sources on mindfulness, compassion-based therapies such as acceptance and commitment therapy (Hayes, 2004) and the literature on stress management. The references given in the reference list are general ones, but you will find variations on many of these exercises in the citations listed.

Meditation 1. Cultivating an internal quiet space

As for all of these meditations, the first step is to find yourself a place where you can be physically reasonably comfortable and free from disturbances. Your desk will do, or a quiet room at work or at home. You can sit, stand or lie down; whatever you feel most comfortable with, given the situation. You need about 15 minutes for this exercise. The instructions are really simple: position yourself comfortably and then – if you are happy to do so – close your eyes. Deliberately start to slow down your breathing and breathe as deeply and slowly as you can comfortably manage. That's it! Stop after 5–10 minutes at first and develop your ability to do this up to a duration of 10–15 minutes.

While you are doing this, you may find all kinds of sensations, thoughts and other distractions occurring both internally and externally. That is fine, and an empty mind with no thoughts is certainly not the aim here, so don't concern yourself if you experience many distractions, even uncomfortable ones. These are all part of the experience. Your attitude should just be one of mild curiosity. While you maintain your breathing, perhaps you could observe what physical sensations, environmental sounds and other distractions occur. You could just observe with curiosity what happens when a thought occurs; for instance, you might find yourself engaging with some of your thoughts until they become elaborate trains of worry, extensive to-do lists, or just a plethora of memories, plans, images and so forth. Do not expect this to be a comfortable experience. The aim of the exercise is to begin to really pay attention and observe your mind and your body with an attitude of curiosity, a little like a scientist studying your subjective experiences.

Meditation 2. Body scan

Start off with a few minutes of Meditation 1, above. Then focus your attention on the tips of your toes. What sensations do you feel there? Are you aware of feeling hot or cold, itchy or comfortable? Gently shift your awareness upwards through your body until you get to the top your head. For each segment of your body, try to study any sensations you might experience there. This meditation is called a body scan and you can do this very slowly or quite fast, continually crafting your awareness of your body and how you fit into your own skin. Keep it up for anywhere between 1 and 15 minutes; however long you can manage. As you repeatedly practise this meditation, you are likely to find it easier with time, and you may be able to sustain the body scan for longer. Once you are able to sustain your attention on your body for an extended period of time, say 10 minutes or more, you might want to expand this exercise in either of the following ways: you could do a number of body scans in succession or, alternatively, you could practise intensifying your focus on one area at a time. Try to notice any "signals" your body is emitting that don't normally reach your awareness.

For the body scan meditation, there is one caveat, however. It is extremely important that every time you do this exercise, you ensure that when you notice any sensation or signal from inside your body, you refrain from interpreting it. Just noticing is enough for now! There are two reasons for this: Firstly, the body scan is a mindfulness exercise – in other words, it is designed to help you craft awareness of your interoceptive sensations (sensations emanating from inside your body). Mindfulness is about awareness in the present moment with *acceptance.* So, whatever signals arise, they are tolerated and experienced as part of each present moment as the moment arises. The second reason is that some body signals can easily be misinterpreted. If you find that your body scan causes you this kind of distress, please do not continue with this particular meditation – there are others listed here that may be similarly effective in helping you focus your awareness.

In this exercise you deal with distractions in exactly the same way as above: just let them be, and observe with curiosity what your mind tends to do with them – even if that means that you teach yourself to live with (tolerate) some degree of annoyance.

Meditation 3. Thought awareness

This meditation builds on the previous two exercises. The first step is to complete a few body scans, or if you prefer, spend about 5 minutes just sitting quietly in a relaxed position.

Remain in your relaxed position and start focusing your awareness on the thoughts, images and sensations that pop into your mind.

The key instruction is not to *engage* with any of the mental events you experience, just to notice them and pay them no more attention than if they were drops of rain falling from the sky.

This means that if a worry comes into your mind, just note that it is a worry. Not engaging with the worry means that you do not respond to the worry with an internal dialogue. Pretend you are in a conversation with someone else and it is their turn to talk. The thought, image or worry is what they had to say, so to speak, and that you have chosen to hear them out, but not to respond. Let the worry pass, noting what it is, just as you would remember what the other person might have said with a view to your response in your next conversational turn, yet you let the next idea or thought come in and go out again. Do the same again, a thousand times if needed.

If a task from your to-do list pops into your mind, the aim is to note it, but not to complete the list. You can always do that afterwards.

Initially, some people find this exercise easier if, at the start, they keep a pad and pen with them and note down any trains of thought that need to be completed later on. Except for the very first few times you try this, I do not generally recommend this practice as it has the potential to function as a distraction from crafting awareness.

At the start, many people find that they engage with a train of thought even before they can stop themselves, as this is such a difficult habit to break. As soon as you realise you've turned a thought into a web of planning or worry, stop and wait for the next thought – you won't have to wait long! Disengage from trains of thought, even if they are already well under way. Stop them in their tracks without completing them; next time you may catch yourself earlier in the process of engaging with your mental processes and stop yourself falling into this trap sooner. It is difficult, but persist with practising this technique. It is one of the most essential compassion skills to learn: awareness with acceptance and then letting go.

The body and thought awareness meditations described above are really powerful, but surprisingly difficult to master. It might help you to think of these as follows. Each exercise generally consists of three parts: the first is to physically and mentally relax by finding a comfortable physical location to be in, a relaxed body posture and to actively breathe fully and deeply. Secondly, there is the process of paying attention. A helpful metaphor springs to mind here, namely that of a searchlight. As you pay attention to different aspects of your environment, mental life or physical sensations, it is as if you are aiming a beam of light at that aspect of the neural signals that are generated inside your brain.

The third part of these exercises consists of tuning into the various thoughts, sensations or experiences that are the topic of each of the different meditations. Think of this as tuning in an old-fashioned radio – you might have to spend some time gently twisting the dial, and, in the process, tolerate bursts of irritating background noise, but once the station you are seeking is tuned in, the signal comes through loud and clear. If, after some time, the tuning drifts off, clarity and focus can be restored by careful retuning.

Meditations 4 and 5. The compassionate other and self-compassion

Once you have managed to disengage from mental trains of thought, as outlined in the previous meditation, you could move on to more directly cultivating the subjective elements of compassion. For example, you could spend some time visualising someone who has showed you compassion or kindness without personal gain. It could be a very small or a very substantial compassionate deed.

After replaying the compassionate episode in your imagination, try to focus your attention on the person who was compassionate towards you. Try to visualise their compassion as a flow of energy from them directed towards you. Feel the warmth, kindness, and joy contained within that compassionate field. Stay with that feeling and let it percolate through your mind and then through your whole body.

During a subsequent meditation, you could repeat the above exercise and, at the end, visualise yourself reflecting that very same compassion you experienced from the compassionate other back onto yourself. Generate that same warmth and kindness towards yourself. In particular, bring to mind all those aspects of yourself you usually judge negatively, dislike, or even wish to disown. Your self-compassion is not complete until you are able to shine this imaginary ray of compassionate light fully on even the darkest corner of your inner self. Compassion is unconditional and self-compassion should be too.

Meditation 6. Crafting compassionate intent towards a friend and an enemy

You can continue to develop the previous exercise by bringing to mind a good friend and shining your compassion onto them. The aim would be to work towards crafting real compassionate intent, as described above. Wishing your friend to be well, happy and healthy is a good place to start. However, compassionate intent includes developing an action orientation which might mean that for you, compassion towards a friend would translate into compassionate action.

Compassion towards a friend is quite easy for many people and a good place to start with turning the warm emotions generated by compassionate feelings into action, but of course, compassion stretches us and impels us to grow and mature. From compassion towards a friend, revisit the self-compassion exercise above, this time making an effort to bring compassionate intent towards the self in play. How would you translate self-compassion into self-kindness without engaging in self-indulgence and actions that might even damage you? (For instance, unbridled comfort eating might feel very good, but is likely to be damaging to your health and your mental health in the long term!)

The challenge of self-compassion does not represent the end of the journey, though. What about compassionate intent towards your enemies: those who actively seek to do you harm, but also those who dislike you, who judge you, or perhaps those you judge and dislike. What would a compassionate stance towards those people look like for you? Compassionate practice might start with visualising your own compassion like a ray of warm sunshine that you direct toward your enemies, wishing even them well – but it cannot end there. Compassion craves action – which in this context will be a very substantial challenge for most people. A short anecdote from the life of Gandhi illustrates this point: while in prison in South Africa for contravening race laws, he hand-made a pair of sandals for the prime minister of the country at the time, and thus enacted his compassionate intent even towards the man ultimately responsible for his incarceration.

Meditation 7. The universal smile

This visualisation meditation comes from the practice of Qigong, an ancient tradition that is currently gaining prevalence as a holistic approach to stress management (Chen, 2007).

While in a relaxed state of mind (see Meditations 1–3, above) start to visualise a small image of yourself with a smile in the centre of your forehead. Take a moment to feel the warmth and kindness that emanate from your smile. Now slowly grow your smile, allowing it to permeate your mind and cover your entire face.

Let your smile grow even more to fill your body. Let every fibre of your being smile in harmony. Imagine this smile that is now emanating from you growing until it reaches beyond your body, covering and filling the room you are in and anyone else who may be within it. Grow it still more until it covers the entire building, street, town and country you are in. Imagine your smile growing to cover the whole earth, the solar system and beyond. Let your smile grow even further until it covers the entire universe, permeating everything with warmth and kindness.

Stay with that image for a moment, before you slowly bring back your smile from the boundless universe, down onto this planet, your city or town, the building and room you are in, and finally, your own body – all the while staying in touch with its permeating warmth and kindness. Finally, let it settle back on your forehead and remain there just as you originally visualised it. This is the universal smile, and also your smile.

REFERENCES

Bornemann, B., and Singer, T. (2013) A cognitive neuroscience perspective: the resource Model. In: Singer, T. & Bolz, M. (eds) Compassion: bridging practice and science. (ebook) Munich, Germany: Max Planck Society (pp. 179–191).

Buber, M. (1937) *I and Thou*. Edinburgh: T & T Clark.

Chen, K. (2007) Qigong therapy for stress management. In: Lehrer, P., Woolfolk, R. & Sime, L. (eds) *Principles and Practice of Stress Management* (3rd ed). New York: The Guilford Press (pp. 428–448).

Darley, J. & Batson, D. (1973) "From Jerusalem to Jericho": a study of situational and dispositional variables in helping behaviour. *Journal of Personality and Social Psychology*, **27(1):** 100–108.

Francis, R. (2013) *Report of the Mid Staffordshire NHS Foundation Trust Public Inquiry (vols. 1–3)*. London: The Stationery Office.

Gilbert, P. (2010) *Training our minds in, with, and for compassion*. Downloadable resource available from www.compassionatemind.co.uk.

Hangartner, D. (2013) Human suffering and four immeasurables. In: Singer, T. & Bolz, M. (eds) *Compassion: bridging practice and science*. (ebook) Munich, Germany: Max Planck Society (pp. 153–164).

Hayes, S. C. (2004) Acceptance and commitment therapy, relational frame theory, and the third wave of behavioral and cognitive therapies. *Behavior Therapy*, **35(4):** 639–665.

Jinananda (Duncan Steen) (2012) *Meditating: a Buddhist view.* Cambridge: Windhorse Publications.

Kabat-Zinn, J. (1982) An outpatient program in behavioral medicine for chronic pain patients based on the practice of mindfulness meditation: theoretical considerations and preliminary results. *General Hospital Psychiatry, 4:* 33–47.

Kabat-Zinn, J. (1994) *Wherever you go, there you are: mindfulness meditation in everyday life.* New York: Hyperion.

Klimecki, O., Ricard, M. & Singer, T. (2013) Empathy versus compassion – lessons from 1st and 3rd person methods. In Singer, T. & Bolz, M. (eds.) *Compassion: bridging practice and science.* (ebook) Munich, Germany: Max Planck Society (pp. 273–287).

Maslach, C. (1982) *Burnout – the cost of caring.* Englewood Cliffs, New Jersey: Prentice Hall.

Menzies-Lyth, I. (1990) Social systems as a defence against anxiety: an empirical study of the nursing service of a general hospital. In: Trist, E. & Murray, H. (eds) *The social engagement of social science: a Tavistock anthology.* London: Free Association Books (pp. 439–462).

Neff, K. & Germer, C. (2013) Being kind to yourself – the science of self-compassion. Chapter 16 in: Singer, T. & Bolz, M. (eds.) *Compassion: bridging practice and science.* (ebook) Munich, Germany: Max Planck Society (pp. 290–312).

NHS Commissioning Board (2012) *Compassion in practice. Nursing Midwifery and Care Staff. Our vision and strategy.* London: Department of Health.

Rao, S. (2015) *Are YOU ready to succeed?: unconventional strategies for achieving personal mastery in business and life.* CreateSpace Independent Publishing Platform.

Stephens, P. (2013) *Social Pedagogy: heart and head*. Bremen: EHV.

Stokoe, P. (2011) The healthy and the unhealthy organisation: how can we help teams remain effective? Chapter 13 in: Rubitel, A. & Reiss, D. (eds) *Containment in the Community: supportive frameworks for thinking about antisocial behaviour and mental health* (pp. 237–260). London: Karnac Books.

Teasdale, J., Segal, Z. & Williams, J. (1995) How does cognitive therapy prevent relapse and why should attentional control (mindfulness) training help? *Behavior Research and Therapy*, **33:** 225–239.

ALSO OF INTEREST....

Developing Reflective Practice is an essential companion for practitioners and students in health and social care who wish, or need, to incorporate reflective practice into their workplace.

The material in this book is suitable for students and practitioners in a variety of fields, including nursing, psychology, social work, therapeutic child care, and education. What all of these fields have in common is that practitioners deal with fundamental human needs such as physical and mental health, housing, and education.

Students on placement as well as qualified and experienced practitioners can benefit from reading this book and working through the reflective exercises that accompany the text.

The goal of the book is to help the reader feel confident and competent when confronted with complex and emotionally demanding situations in the workplace. By working through the numerous and varied activities and exercises detailed in this book, the reader will acquire the skills needed to make sense of their experiences in a professional context.

'...an excellent introduction for staff who are starting out their exploration of reflective practice... this concise and creative publication will be invaluable in integrated settings to support safe and ethical service provision in health and social care.'

— Journal of Social Work

'In this book the clinical psychologist Natius Oelofsen describes the processes of learning and the three-step reflective cycle, explaining how keeping a reflective journal offers insights into self and behaviour, and using critical analysis to reflect on even ordinary, everyday incidents... There is so much in this book, including getting the most from supervision, ethical issues and dealing with work-based stress, as well as exercises, activities and case examples.'

— Nursing Standard